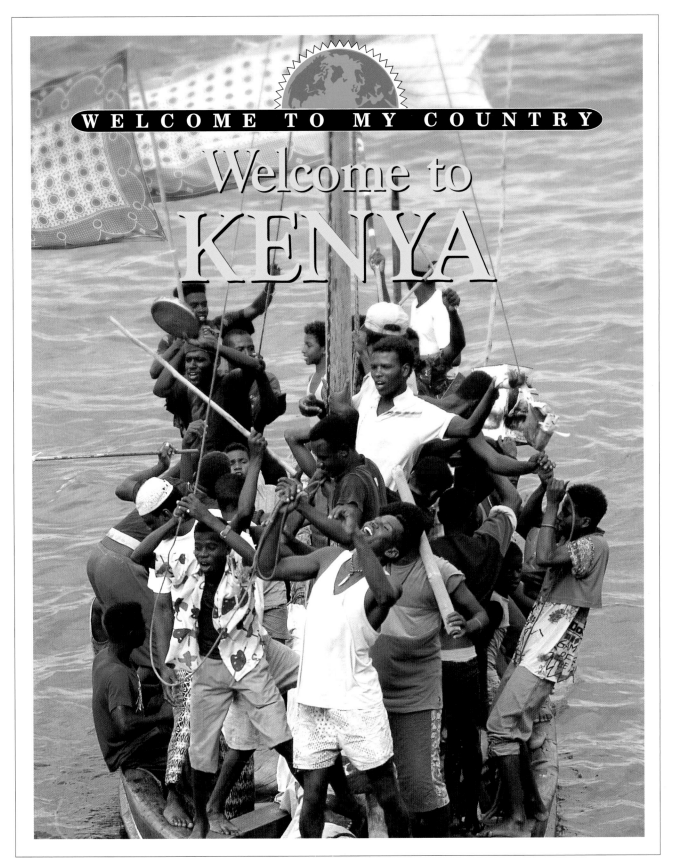

WELCOME TO MY COUNTRY

Welcome to
KENYA

FRANKLIN WATTS
LONDON • SYDNEY

PICTURE CREDITS
AFP: 33
Michele Burgess: 3 (bottom), 7 (bottom),
    9, 24
Camera Press: 3 (top), 13, 14, 15 (all)
Camerapix: 29 (bottom)
Victor Englebert: 2, 3 (centre), 6, 7 (top), 8,
    16, 23 (top)
Focus Team — Italy: 4, 41
Haga Library: 20, 28, 30
HBL Network Photo Agency: 5, 45
The Hutchison Library: 18, 22, 25
The Image Bank: 43
International Photobank: 21, 32
Björn Klingwall: 40
Jason Lauré: 17, 27, 29 (top), 31, 36, 37,
    38, 39
Lonely Planet Images: cover
Nik Wheeler: 10
Chip Peterson: 1, 34
photolibrary.com: 23
Peter Sanders: 35
Liba Taylor: 19
Topham Picturepoint: 11, 12, 26

Digital Scanning by Superskill Graphics Pte Ltd

This edition first published in 2006 by
Franklin Watts
338 Euston Road
London NW1 3BH

This edition is published for sale only in the United Kingdom and Eire.

© Marshall Cavendish International (Asia) Pte Ltd 2006
Originated and designed by Times Editions–Marshall Cavendish
An imprint of Marshall Cavendish International (Asia) Pte Ltd
1 New Industrial Road, Singapore 536196

Written by: Roseline NgCheong-Lum & Victoria Derr
Designer: Lock Hong Liang
Picture researchers: Thomas Khoo & Joshua Ang

A CIP catalogue record for this book
is available from the British Library.

ISBN-10: 0 7496 7017 7
ISBN-13: 978 0 7496 7017 7

Printed in Malaysia

Franklin Watts is a division of Hachette Children's Books.

Contents

Words that appear in the glossary are printed in **bold** the first time they occur in the text.

Welcome to Kenya!

The Republic of Kenya is a country on the eastern coast of Africa. It lies on the Equator. Kenya is home to many tropical plants and wild animals. Kenyans belong to various **tribes**, but they all speak English or **Swahili**. Let's explore the beautiful country of Kenya and learn all about its amazing people.

Opposite: These gigantic tusks across Moi Avenue in Mombasa are made of fibreglass.

Below: Nairobi is the capital of Kenya. The city bustles with activity.

The Flag of Kenya

The Kenyan flag consists of red, black and green bands, with a shield and two crossed spears in the centre. Black represents the people, red symbolises the struggle for independence, and green signifies Kenya's natural resources.

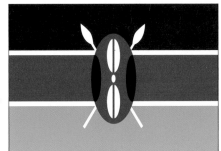

The Land

Kenya is more than twice the size of the United Kingdom. The eastern part of the country borders the Indian Ocean. The capital is Nairobi, which means "place of cold waters". Other important Kenyan towns are Mombasa, on the coast, and Kisumu, near Lake Victoria.

Left: Salt has formed on the banks of the Suguta River in the Great Rift Valley.

Outstanding Natural Features

Northern Kenya is mainly desert, whereas the western side is dominated by **savanna**, or dry grassland. The Great Rift Valley separates the savanna from the rest of Kenya. A large population of wild animals lives in the valley, which contains many **extinct** volcanoes and eight beautiful lakes.

Above: Termites build nests of compacted soil that can rise higher than a house.

Left: The endangered African elephant roams freely in the Samburu Game Reserve.

Hundreds of interesting plants and animals live in Kakamega Forest on the western edge of the country. Snowcapped Mt. Kenya is the highest mountain in the country. The longest river is the Tana River.

A Tropical Climate

Kenya has two seasons: wet and dry. The wet season is cool, and the dry season can be very hot. The coastal region is hot and humid, while the north is hot and dry. Very little rain falls in the southeast. The highlands are cooler than the rest of Kenya, and the soil is very fertile. Most Kenyans live in the southwest, where the climate is cool and rainfall is plentiful.

Below: Few plants grow in the savanna of northeastern Kenya. One **exception** is the flat-topped **acacia.**

Wildlife Kingdom

The Kenyan savanna is home to many animals, including hippopotamuses, lions, leopards, elephants, zebras, giraffes and rhinoceroses. Fish and crocodiles live in the rivers and lakes. Birds live in the wetlands, as well as in the forested areas.

The preservation of so many species of animals poses a major challenge. Many animals are threatened by diseases, hunting and loss of habitat.

History

Thousands of years ago, there were four groups of people in Kenya: the **hunter-gatherers**, Cushites, Bantu and Nilotes. The first visitors were Indonesian traders who arrived in about 500 BCE. The Arabs arrived 1,000 years later. Between 1500 and 1700, Kenyan tribes fought among themselves for land, cattle and slaves.

Below: Buildings constructed by Arab settlers now lie in ruins along the Kenyan coast.

British East Africa

In the nineteenth century, Britain and Germany fought over East Africa. Both countries sent expeditions to explore the inner regions. Kenya, Uganda and Tanzania were soon divided between Britain and Germany. In 1895, the British assumed the administration of the area from the coast of Kenya to the Great Rift Valley. This territory was called the British East Africa **Protectorate**. The country changed its name to Kenya Colony, after Mt. Kenya, in 1920.

Fight for Independence

Many British settlers moved into Kenya and established farms in the fertile regions around Mt. Kenya. This pushed native tribes into smaller and less fertile areas. In the 1940s, the Kenyans, led by Jomo Kenyatta, became very unhappy with their living conditions. The **Mau Mau** Rebellion, from 1952 to 1956, showed the British that the Kenyan people were determined to obtain independence.

Left: John Ndisi, Kenya's first secretary (*left*), and JN Karanja, high commissioner (*right*), launched the new Kenyan flag on 12 December 1963 at Kenya House in London.

"Pulling Together"

Kenya became an independent nation in 1963, with Kenyatta as prime minister. In 1964, Kenyatta was made Kenya's first president when it became a republic. Calling on the various tribes to "pull together", he led the country towards economic progress and political stability. Kenyatta was very popular because he helped improve the lives of the people.

Above: Supporters of Jomo Kenyatta make their way to the presidential palace following Kenyatta's 1973 re-election. Daniel arap Moi, then vice president and Minister for Home Affairs, is in the front row (*third from right*).

Tribal Struggles

Kenyatta died in 1978 and Daniel arap Moi became president. He favoured his own tribe, the Kalenjin. In 1982, some members of the military tried to remove him by force, but the rebellion failed. The president then imposed even tighter rules on the country. In 1992, however, Moi was pressured into giving more rights to the people.

Below: In 1978, after he was installed as president of Kenya, Daniel arap Moi inspects a guard of honour.

Jomo Kenyatta (c. 1894–1978)

Kenyatta received his education from Scottish missionaries. When Kenya became independent in 1963, Kenyatta became its first prime minister. He was president from 1964 until his death in 1978.

Jomo Kenyatta

Wangari Maathai (1940–)

Wangari Maathai was the first woman in Kenya to become a professor at the University of Nairobi. She started the Green Belt Movement in 1977 to protect the natural environment of Kenya by planting trees. She won the Nobel Peace Prize in 2004.

Wangari Maathai

Richard Leakey (1944–)

Richard Leakey discovered many human **fossils** in Kenya. They show that people lived there a very long time ago. He is active in wildlife preservation and the protection of the country's natural parks.

Richard Leakey

Government and the Economy

Government

The head of state is the president, who is also commander-in-chief of the armed forces. Various ministries look into the different aspects of the government. All ministers report to the president.

Left: The National Assembly meets at the parliament building in Nairobi.

The People's Representatives

There are eight provinces in Kenya. Representatives from these provinces make up the National Assembly. There are more than 200 representatives, most of whom are elected every five years. In recent years, women have been well represented in the National Assembly. Kenyan laws are a combination of British, tribal and Islamic laws.

Above: Kenyans believe strongly in the **democratic** process and play an active part in election campaigns.

Fishing and Farming

A large number of Kenyans are fishermen and farmers. The rivers and the sea yield many fish. Much of the catch is processed before it is exported.

Most of Kenya's farms are situated in the highlands. Farmers grow **millet**, corn, beans, yams, cassavas and bananas. They also raise cattle. Crops grown for export include tobacco, cotton, coffee, tea and **pyrethrum**.

Below: Tea grows abundantly in the Kenyan highlands.

Natural Resources and Tourism

Kenya has many natural resources, such as gold, limestone, rubies, soda ash and **garnets**. Tourists on **safari** trips contribute a large amount of revenue to the economy.

Left: Most of the factories in Kenya rely on people rather than machinery to produce goods. In this picture, women make bead jewellery for export.

Trade

Kenya imports heavy equipment, machinery and manufactured goods. Most of its exports are agricultural products, such as coffee, tea, **sisal**, pyrethrum and flowers. Kenya's main trading partners are African, European and Middle Eastern countries.

People and Lifestyle

The Kenyan people belong to a variety of tribes divided into three families: Bantu, Cushite and Nilote. The Bantu tribes include the Kisii, Kikuyu, Luhya, Kamba and Meru. The Maasai, Turkana, Samburu, Kalenjin and Luo are Nilotic people. Cushitic people belong to the Somali, Boran, Rendille and Oromo tribes. Kenya's minorities include Arabs, Indians and Europeans.

Below: Most Kikuyu are farmers. Their tribe was among the first to adopt the Western style of dress.

Left: Maasai women wear very elaborate necklaces made of many strands of small, colourful beads.

The Tribes

The Kikuyu tribe is one of the main tribes in Kenya. This tribe lives in the highlands. The people are skilled weavers and blacksmiths. Another Bantu tribe is the Swahili. Most Swahili are farmers or fishermen. They are also very good at wood carving, weaving and metalwork. Swahili is one of Kenya's two national languages. One of Kenya's best-known tribes is the Maasai, a small tribe famous for its fierceness in battle.

Clans

The family is the foundation of social life in Kenya. Families are grouped into clans, and several clans form a tribe. Many tribes have similar customs and ceremonies. When a child is born, the family holds a naming ceremony to ensure that the **legacy** of the clan is passed down to the next generation. Warrior tribes also hold **initiation ceremonies** for young boys.

Above: Family is very important to the Kikuyu.

Women

Most women in rural areas spend their days gathering wood, carrying water and planting crops. They are responsible for all the household chores and for raising the children.

Urban Families

Many Kenyan families living in the city prefer a Western lifestyle, but clan matters are still very important to tribal Kenyans in the cities. Many Arab and Asian Kenyans live in towns.

Education

Education in Kenya consists of primary and secondary school and university. Children learn history, mathematics, English and literature. Most lessons are conducted in English. Students also participate in sports at school, mainly football and rugby.

Most children attend primary and secondary school. Very few go on to a university because there are few schools.

Below: Kenyan children learn their lessons in English.

Literacy

Kenyans are totally committed to education. Four out of five Kenyans can read and write in English or Swahili. Kenya has one of the highest rates of **literacy** in Africa. The Kenyan education ministry still has a lot of work to do, however. More people need to be given an opportunity to attend a university. Women, especially those in rural communities, are still not getting as much opportunity to learn as men.

Religious Beliefs

Most Kenyans are Christians. A small number are Muslims, mainly the Arabs and Asians. The Maasai and Samburu follow their tribal religious beliefs. Although they are Christians, many Kenyans also believe in tribal myths and a single god. They believe that *Ngai* (en-GAI), a supreme being, created the universe and lives in heaven or on high mountains.

Tribal Observances

Many tribes believe in ancestor spirits. The Kikuyu and Kamba talk to their ancestors and offer them food and drink. The Maasai think their spiritual leaders are reborn as snakes when they die. For this reason, the Maasai do not kill snakes. The Kamba call on Ngai in times of great distress, such as during droughts. They offer sacrifices to Ngai for help.

Below: Muslims celebrate Prophet Muhammad's birthday with a mock fight. Many Muslims live along the coast of Kenya.

Language

Both English and Swahili are spoken in Kenya. Most Kenyans learn English at school, although they do not speak it at home. Each tribe or ethnic group also has its own language.

Although it is derived from Arabic, Swahili is written with Roman letters. Swahili sounds very different from English. Many words begin with the letters *n* and *g*, making the sound come from the back of the mouth.

Opposite: Uhuru Park is a centre for cultural activities in Nairobi.

Left: A sign in the Nairobi Arboretum Forest Reserve lists the rules in English (*left*), Swahili (*centre*), and Arabic (*right*).

Kenyan Literature

Swahili writers focus on folk tales, mysteries and stories relating to the struggles of the 1950s and 1960s. Important Swahili writers include James Mbotel, Ali Jemaadar Amir and Katama Mkangi.

James Ngugi was the first East African writer to publish a novel in English. He usually writes about the struggles of the Kenyan people.

Below: James Ngugi is one of the most famous writers in Kenya.

Arts

Kenyan artisans are among the best in the world. Many household items are beautifully decorated. The Maasai put colourful beads around tall milk containers. The Swahili make intricately carved doors and weave coconut fibres into household items. The Kamba carve wildlife statues from wood.

Below: Maasai artists obtain their paints from the earth. They use clay to make whites and yellows. They mix the clay with the juice of the wild nightshade plant to produce red.

Soapstone Art

The Kisii use soapstone, a pinkish white stone from quarries in western Kenya, for carving. They make bowls, vases, candlesticks and pipes. One of the most well-known soapstone items is the "Kisii stool", a low seat covered with colourful beads. The Kisii also apply a powder made of ground soapstone to their faces for ceremonies, such as initiations and funerals.

Above: Wood-carvers make a good living in Kenya. Carvings of African wildlife are exported to Europe and North America.

Dances

Kenyan tribes dance to mark an event or a ceremony. The music is provided by drums, shakers and flutes. Children have their own dances that prepare them for the adult dances. As they grow up, they have to master a set number of dances before they can try the maiden or warrior dances of the adults. Kikuyu women can choose their dance partners.

Above: Wearing animal skins and adorned with body paint, Kikuyu men and women perform a traditional dance.

Building Styles

In Swahili towns, houses are built very close to each other so that people can easily communicate with their neighbours. Along the coast, especially in Mombasa and Lamu, houses are made of coral. Hard coral goes into the foundations and walls, while soft coral is carved into decorative **motifs**. In Lamu, beautiful patterns of flowers or leaves decorate the doors.

Below: The doorway of this guesthouse in Lamu is carved into the shape of a flower.

Leisure

Most Kenyans work very hard and do not have much time for leisure. People in the countryside try to combine work and leisure. Women work together and communicate at that time. Farmers sing while they cultivate their land.

Left: In *kigogo* (ki-GO-go), the players try to capture their opponent's pieces by moving their counters around a board.

Tea-time

Many Kenyans like to have a cup of tea at around 4 pm. A tea break is a good opportunity to spend time with family and friends.

Leisure in Nairobi

When time is available, people in Nairobi visit markets, museums and art galleries during the day. At night, they may go dancing or watch a film or a play. Most films are imported from the United States, Europe or India. Some film festivals focus on local culture.

Left: The Swahili in Lamu often launch a new boat on a Friday, after the weekly prayers in the mosque. The people chant as they push the boat into the water.

Leaders of the Pack

Athletes from Kenya dominate marathons and long-distance races all over the world. Kenyan men have won the London Marathon every year from 2004 to 2006. Since 1964, Kenyan athletes have won 17 Olympic gold medals.

Kenyan women are also good athletes but have not received much support. Most female runners stop running to marry and have children.

Above: Kenyan athletes are among the best in the world. Children start training at a young age to build their speed and endurance.

Sport

The most popular sport in Kenya is football. Every weekend, men and boys play the game in parks, village fields or stadiums. Football league matches draw large crowds.

Car racing is gaining popularity, and drivers take part in the Rhino Charge and the Safari Rally. In the cities, people enjoy golf and boating.

Below: Both players and spectators have an exciting time at football matches.

Rites of Passage

Circumcision is an important event in the life of Kenyan boys. It marks their entry into the adult world. Circumcision ceremonies are very elaborate and can last several days. Wearing goatskin capes, the young boys roam the villages, singing. They are led by older men as they gather

Below: A Samburu mother shaves her son's head before circumcision.

wood for bows, arrows and clubs. Before the ceremony, their mothers shave the boys' heads. The circumcision itself is very quick, and the boys show their courage by not crying out.

Above: Former president Moi arrives at Nairobi's Nyayo Stadium during the Kenyatta Day celebrations.

National Holidays

Independence Day falls on 12 December and is marked by parades. Kenyatta Day, on 20 October, is another important festival. It marks the British arrest of Jomo Kenyatta in 1953 during the Mau Mau Rebellion.

Food

The Kenyan diet is composed mainly of starchy foods, vegetables and some meat. The main foods are potatoes, rice, millet, sorghum, cassavas, yams and corn. These are either cooked on their own or mixed with spices and meat. Kenyans also eat a lot of vegetables and fruits. Meals are served on a large platter, and everyone eats from the same dish.

Left: A Maasai woman stirs a pot of *ugali* (OO-gahl-ee), while her children watch and learn.

Kenyan Dishes

One of the most popular Kenyan dishes is ugali. It consists of cornmeal mixed with water and salt. Ugali is eaten with vegetables or, during special occasions, with meat. Kenyans like spicy foods, and curries are often eaten with rice. Some dishes use coconut milk. A spicy bean and coconut milk stew is eaten with rice or porridge. Chicken mixed with coconut milk and various spices is also eaten with rice.

Above: Most towns and villages have an open market where fresh fruit and vegetables are sold.

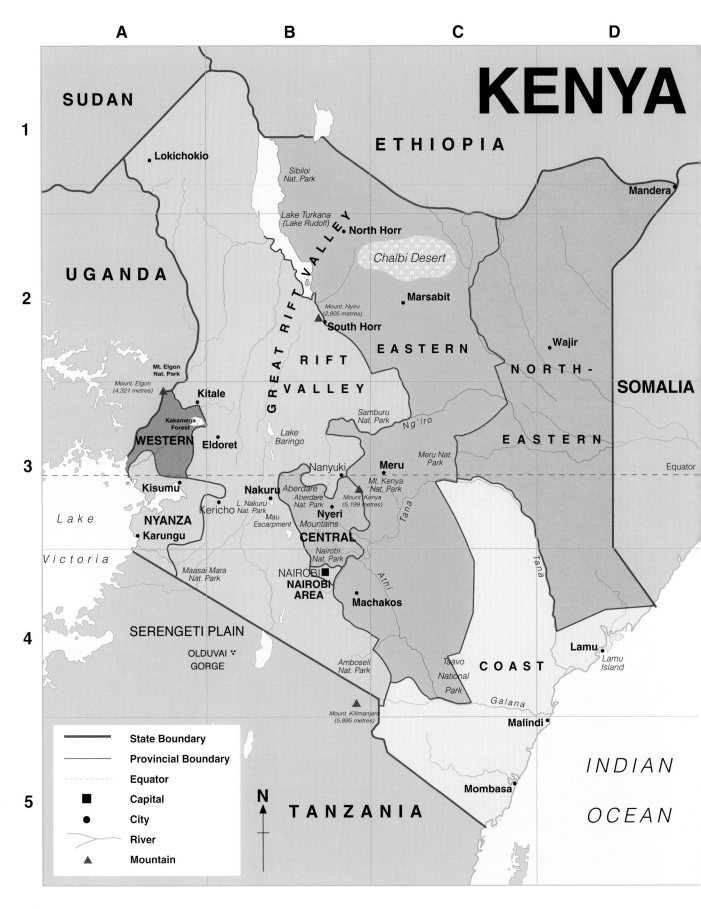

KENYA

SUDAN

ETHIOPIA

• Lokichokio

Sibiloi Nat. Park

Lake Turkana (Lake Rudolf)

• North Horr

Chalbi Desert

UGANDA

• Marsabit

Mount. Nyiru (2,805 metres)

• South Horr

• Wajir

EASTERN

N O R T H -

Mt. Elgon Nat. Park

Mount. Elgon (4,321 metres)

• Kitale

Kakamega Forest

WESTERN

• Eldoret

Lake Baringo

Samburu Nat. Park

Ng'iro

E A S T E R N

Meru Nat. Park

SOMALIA

Nanyuki •

Meru

R I F T

V A L L E Y

G R E A T   R I F T   V A L L E Y

Equator

• Kisumu

Nakuru

L. Nakuru Nat. Park

Aberdare Aberdare Nat. Park

Mount. Kenya (5,199 metres)

NYANZA

Kericho •

Mau Escarpment

Nyeri

Mt. Kenya Nat. Park

Tana

Nyeri Mountains

• Karungu

CENTRAL

Nairobi Nat. Park

Lake

Victoria

NAIROBI ■

NAIROBI AREA

Athi

Machakos

Tana

SERENGETI PLAIN

Maasai Mara Nat. Park

OLDUVAI ☙ GORGE

Amboseli Nat. Park

Tsavo National Park

C O A S T

Lamu •

Lamu Island

Galana

▲ *Mount Kilimanjaro (5,895 metres)*

Malindi •

INDIAN

Mombasa •

OCEAN

N

T A N Z A N I A

▬▬▬	State Boundary
───	Provincial Boundary
- - -	Equator
■	Capital
●	City
∼	River
▲	Mountain

42

Above: Animals gather at a waterhole in Tsavo National Park.

Athi River C4

Central Province B3
Chalbi Desert C2
Coast Province C4

Eastern Province C2
Ethiopia C1

Great Rift Valley
 B2–B3

Indian Ocean D5

Kakamega Forest
 A3
Kisumu A3

Lake Nakuru B3

Lake Turkana B1–B2
Lake Victoria A3–A4
Lamu D4

Mombasa C5
Mt. Elgon A3
Mt. Kenya B3
Mt. Kilimanjaro B4

Nairobi B4
Nairobi Area
 Province B4
Nakuru B3
Ng'iro River C3
North Eastern
 Province D2–D3
Nyanza Province A3

Olduvai Gorge B4

Rift Valley Province
 B2

Samburu National
 Park C3
Serengeti Plain
 A4–B4
Somalia D2–D3
Sudan A1

Tana River C3–D4
Tanzania B5
Tsavo National Park
 C4

Uganda A2

Western Province
 A3

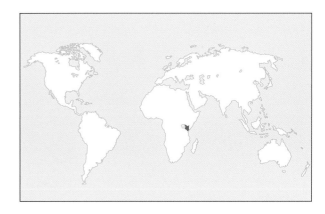

Quick Facts

Official Name	Republic of Kenya
Capital	Nairobi
Official Language	English
National Language	Swahili
Population	34,707,817 (2006 estimate)
Land Area	582,649 square kilometres
Provinces	Central, Coast, Eastern, Nairobi Area, North Eastern, Nyanza, Rift Valley, Western
Highest Point	Mt. Kenya (5,199 metres)
Major River	Tana River
Main Tribes	Kalenjin, Kamba, Kikuyu, Luhya, Luo
Famous Leaders	Jomo Kenyatta (c. 1894–1978); Wangari Maathai (1940–); Thomas Mboya (1930–1969); Daniel arap Moi (1924–); Oginga Odinga (c. 1911–1994)
Major Cities	Kisumu, Mombasa, Nairobi, Nakuru
Currency	Kenyan shilling (92.28 KES = 1 Euro in 2006)

Opposite: Modern office buildings dominate the business district in Nairobi.

Glossary

acacia: a thorny, flat-topped tree usually found in the savanna.

circumcision: the removal of parts of certain sexual organs in males or females.

democratic: relating to the system of government, where the people elect representatives in the government.

exception: a person or object that is not like others in the same category.

extinct: died out; not active anymore.

fossils: the outlines or hardened remains of ancient plants or animals pressed in rock.

garnets: crystalline minerals found in rocks, often used as gems.

hunter-gatherers: people who hunt, fish, or gather wild plants for a living.

initiation ceremonies: rites of acceptance into a certain group.

kigogo (ki-GO-go): a simple game of strategy that involves moving counters around a board to capture the opponent's pieces.

legacy: anything that is passed down from ancestors.

literacy: the ability to read and write.

Mau Mau: a group of people opposed to British rule in Kenya in the 1950s.

millet: the grain of a plant that is used for food.

motifs: repeated designs.

Ngai (en-GAI): the divine spirit of many Kenyan ethnic groups.

protectorate: a country under the protection and partial control of another country.

pyrethrum: a kind of chrysanthemum with red, pink, lilac or white flowers. Dried pyrethrum is used as an insecticide or to cure skin disorders.

safari: an expedition to watch and photograph wild animals, especially in East Africa.

savanna: dry grassland.

sisal: a fibre that is produced by the agave plant.

Swahili: the national language of Kenya, derived from Arabic.

tribes: groups of people with a common origin and culture.

ugali (OO-gahl-ee): a thick porridge made of cornmeal and eaten with vegetables or meat.

More Books to Read

We're from Kenya. Young Explorers series. Vic Parker (Heinemann Library)

Living in Kenya. Ruth Thomson (Franklin Watts)

Kenya. Changing Face of series. Rob Bowden (Hodder Wayland)

Kenya. Letters From Around the World series. Alison Brownlie (Cherrytree Books)

Kenya: Country Insights series. Maierad Maierah Dunne and Wambuli Kairi Eric Nyarjou (Hodder Wayland)

Websites

www.globalgang.org.uk/homeworkhelp/kenya/index.html

www.oxfam.org.uk/coolplanet/kidsweb/world/kenya/index.html

Due to the dynamic nature of the Internet, some websites stay current longer than others. To find additional websites about Kenya, use a reliable search engine and enter one or more of the following. Keywords: *East Africa, Great Rift Valley, Kenyans, Richard Leakey, Maasai, Daniel arap Moi, Nairobi, safari.*

Note to parents and teachers

Every effort has been made by the Publishers to ensure that these websites are suitable for children, that they are of the highest educational value, and that they contain no inappropriate or offensive material. However, because of the nature of the Internet, it is impossible to guarantee that the contents of these sites will not be altered. We strongly advise that Internet access is supervised by a responsible adult.

Index

BW 10/07